MIDLOTHIAN
PUBLIC LIBRARY

DEMCO

Explore the Solar System

Earth and Earth's Moon

WORLD
BOOK

a Scott Fetzer company
Chicago
www.worldbookonline.com

World Book, Inc.
233 N. Michigan Avenue
Chicago, IL 60601
U.S.A.

For information about other World Book publications, visit our Web site at **http://www.worldbookonline.com** or call **1-800-WORLDBK (967-5325).**

For information about sales to schools and libraries, call **1-800-975-3250 (United States),** or **1-800-837-5365 (Canada).**

Library of Congress Cataloging-in-Publication data
Earth and Earth's moon.
    p. cm. -- (Explore the solar system)
    Summary: "An introduction to Earth and its moon for primary and intermediate grade students with information about their features and exploration. Includes charts and diagrams, a list of highlights for each chapter, fun facts, glossary, resource list, and index" -- Provided by publisher.
    Includes index.
    ISBN 978-0-7166-9540-0
    1. Moon--Juvenile literature. 2. Earth--Juvenile literature.
3. Solar system--Juvenile literature. I. World Book, Inc.
    QB582.E245 2011
    523.3--dc22
                                2009038006

ISBN 978-0-7166-9533-2 (set)
Printed in China by Leo Paper Products Ltd.,
    Heshan, Guangdong
1st printing August 2010

Staff
Executive Committee
Vice President and Chief Financial Officer:
  Donald D. Keller
Vice President and Editor in Chief: Paul A. Kobasa
Vice President, Licensing & Business Development:
  Richard Flower
Chief Technology Officer: Tim Hardy
Managing Director, International: Benjamin Hinton
Director, Human Resources: Bev Ecker

Editorial:

Associate Director, Supplementary Publications:
  Scott Thomas
Managing Editor, Supplementary Publications:
  Barbara A. Mayes
Senior Editor, Supplementary Publications:
  Kristina A. Vaicikonis
Manager, Research, Supplementary Publications:
  Cheryl Graham
Manager, Contracts & Compliance
  (Rights & Permissions): Loranne K. Shields
Editor: Michael DuRoss
Writer: Lisa Klobuchar
Indexer: David Pofelski

Graphics and Design:
Manager: Tom Evans
Coordinator, Design Development
  and Production: Brenda B. Tropinski
Senior Designer: Don Di Sante
Contributing Photographs Editor: Carol Parden

Pre-Press and Manufacturing:
Director: Carma Fazio
Manufacturing Manager: Steven K. Hueppchen
Production/Technology Manager: Anne Fritzinger
Proofreader: Emilie Schrage

Picture Acknowledgments:
Cover front: © Allan Davey, Masterfile; Cover back: NASA/JPL-Caltech/UCLA.

© AP Images 45; © Phil Degginger, Alamy Images 25; © Lazlo Podor, Alamy Images 47; © Dreamstime 27; © Calvin J. Hamilton 11, 35; JAXA/NHK 41; NASA 9, 37, 43, 51, 52, 55; NASA/GSFC 20; NASA/JPL 23, 33, 59; NASA/JPL-Caltech 1, 31; NASA/LCROSS 56; NASA/MODIS/GSFC Land Rapid Response Team 15; © Sally Bensusen, Photo Researchers 44; © Mark Garlick, Photo Researchers 49; © Rudiger Lehnen, Photo Researchers 27; SRO/NASA/JPL-Caltech 57; © Shutterstock 38.

WORLD BOOK illustration by Don Di Sante 28, 29; WORLD BOOK illustration by Steve Karp 4; WORLD BOOK illustration by Paul Perreault 7, 17; WORLD BOOK illustration by Roberta Polfus 19; WORLD BOOK illustration by Oxford Illustrators and Don Di Sante 13; WORLD BOOK map 18, 25.

Astronomers use different kinds of photos to learn about objects in space—such as planets. Many photos show an object's natural color. Other photos use false colors. ome false-color images show types of light the human eye cannot normally see. Others have colors that were changed to highlight important features. When appropriate, the captions in this book state whether a photo uses natural or false color.

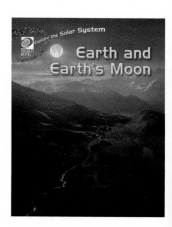

Cover image:
The moon, Earth's only natural satellite, shines down on a river valley in Alaska.

Contents

If a word is printed in **bold letters that look like this,** that word's meaning is given in the glossary on pages 60-61.

Where Is Earth?

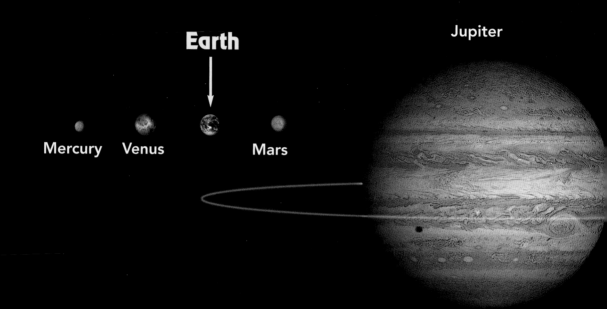

Sun

Mercury Venus **Earth** Mars Jupiter

The **planet** Earth is right under your feet. Earth is also part of the **solar system** and the **universe.**

Within the solar system, Earth is the third planet from the sun. Earth's distance from the sun changes during the **year,** because Earth follows an **elliptical,** or oval-shaped, **orbit** around the sun. On average, Earth is about 93 million miles (150 million kilometers) from the sun.

Earth is one of four planets known to **astronomers** as the inner planets, because they are the closest planets to the sun. The other inner planets are Mercury,

Earth's location in the solar system
(Planets are shown to scale.)

Uranus Neptune

Saturn

Venus, and Mars. They are also known as the *terrestrial* (Earth-like) planets because they are somewhat similar to Earth in composition. All the terrestrial planets consist chiefly of iron and rock. But only Earth has life as we know it.

Earth's orbit is between the orbits of Venus and Mars. Our planet orbits closer to Venus than to any other planet. Earth is only slightly larger than Venus, but it is much larger than Mars or Mercury.

Highlights

- Earth is one of the inner planets of the solar system, the third planet from the sun.
- On average, Earth lies about 93 million miles (150 million kilometers) from the sun.
- Earth orbits the sun between the orbits of Venus and Mars.
- Earth's closest planetary neighbor is Venus.

How Big Is Earth?

Among the **planets** in the **solar system,** Earth is fifth largest in size. Jupiter is the largest planet, followed by Saturn, Uranus (*YUR uh nuhs* or *yu RAY nuhs),* and Neptune.

Earth is much smaller than the sun. About 1 million Earths could fit inside the sun. But Earth is much larger than its **moon.** If Earth's moon were the size of a tennis ball, Earth would be the size of a basketball.

Earth's **diameter** at the **equator** is 7,926 miles (12,756 kilometers). That is the distance straight through the middle of Earth from side to side. Earth's diameter straight through the center from the North Pole to the South Pole is slightly less—about 7,900 miles (12,700 kilometers). Earth bulges slightly at its equator, which is

why its diameter is slightly larger there than between the poles.

Earth's *circumference* (distance around the middle) along the equator is 24,900 miles (40,060 kilometers). The circumference from the North Pole to the South Pole and back again is 24,860 miles (40,010 kilometers). All of Earth's oceans and its continents, islands, and other land masses cover an area that is about 197 million square miles (510 million square kilometers).

Highlights

- Earth is the fifth largest planet in the solar system.
- Earth's diameter at the equator is 7,926 miles (12,756 kilometers).
- About 1 million Earths would fit inside the sun.

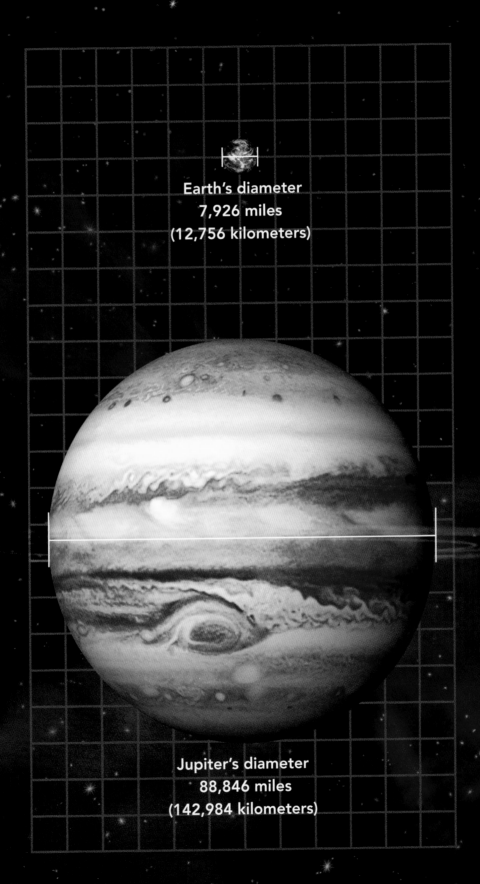

Earth's diameter
7,926 miles
(12,756 kilometers)

Jupiter's diameter
88,846 miles
(142,984 kilometers)

What Does Earth Look Like?

Earth is the only **planet** in the **solar system** with liquid water on its surface. The water makes Earth look blue when viewed from space. This is why Earth is sometimes called "the blue planet." Water covers about 71 percent of Earth's total surface area, or about 140 million

square miles (362 million square kilometers). Clouds in Earth's **atmosphere** appear as white streaks against the blue.

Earth's continents and other land masses appear brownish when viewed from space. About 29 percent of Earth's total surface area, or about 57 million square miles (148 million square kilometers), is covered by land.

Fun Fact

Earth is the only planet in the solar system whose outer layer, or crust, is made up of moving pieces called tectonic plates.

Earth in a
natural-color photo

What Is Earth Made Of?

Much of Earth is made of solid rock. Earth has three layers: the **crust, mantle,** and **core.**

The crust is Earth's thin, cool, outer layer. The crust under the continents is mostly **granite** and similar rock. The crust under the oceans is much thinner. It is mostly **basalt** (*buh SAWLT* or *BAS awlt*), which is a dense and dark volcanic rock. Oxygen is the most common chemical **element** in Earth's crust.

Beneath the crust is the mantle, a thick, hot layer that flows slowly. The crust floats on the mantle like a board on water. Most of the mantle is made up of a group of minerals called **silicates.** They consist of silicon, oxygen, and one or more metallic elements.

The core lies at the center of Earth. The core, which is about the same size as Mars, is made mostly of iron and nickel. Scientists think that the outer part of the core is liquid and that the inner core is solid.

Highlights

- Much of Earth is made of rock, just like the other inner planets.
- Earth's crust under the continents is made mostly of granite. Its crust under the oceans is made mostly of basalt.
- The mantle is made mostly of minerals called silicates, and the core is mostly iron and nickel.

Inside Earth

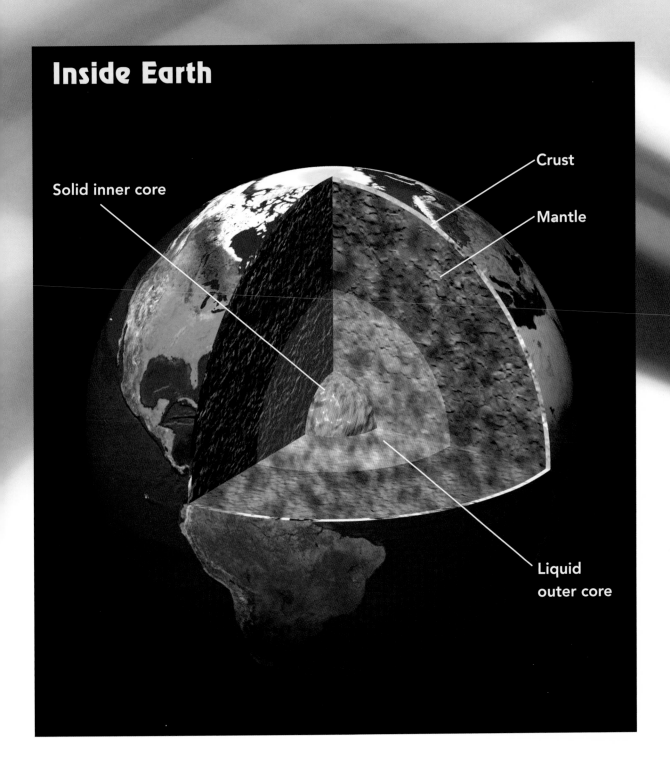

Solid inner core

Crust

Mantle

Liquid outer core

What Is Earth's Atmosphere Like?

Earth is surrounded by a blanket of air called the **atmosphere.** The air becomes thinner the farther you travel from the surface. The atmosphere has no definite upper edge. It fades gradually into space.

The atmosphere consists of four layers. Closest to Earth is the troposphere (TROH puh sfihr). More than three-fourths of the atmosphere's gases are in the troposphere. Earth's plants and animals, including people, live in the troposphere. Nearly all Earth's weather occurs in this layer.

Right above the troposphere is the stratosphere (STRAT uh sfihr or STRAY tuh sfihr). The stratosphere contains most of the atmosphere's ozone (OH zohn). Ozone is a gas that blocks dangerous ultraviolet sunlight from reaching Earth. The highest two layers of the atmosphere are the mesosphere (MEHS uh sfihr or MEE suh sfihr) and thermosphere (THUR muh sfihr). The mesosphere has so little air that airplanes cannot travel there.

Highlights

- Earth is surrounded by a layer of air called the atmosphere.
- Earth's atmosphere is made up of four layers: the troposphere, the stratosphere, the mesosphere, and the thermosphere.
- People live in the troposphere, where most of the gases of the atmosphere are found.
- Most of Earth's weather takes place in the troposphere.

The Layers of the Atmosphere

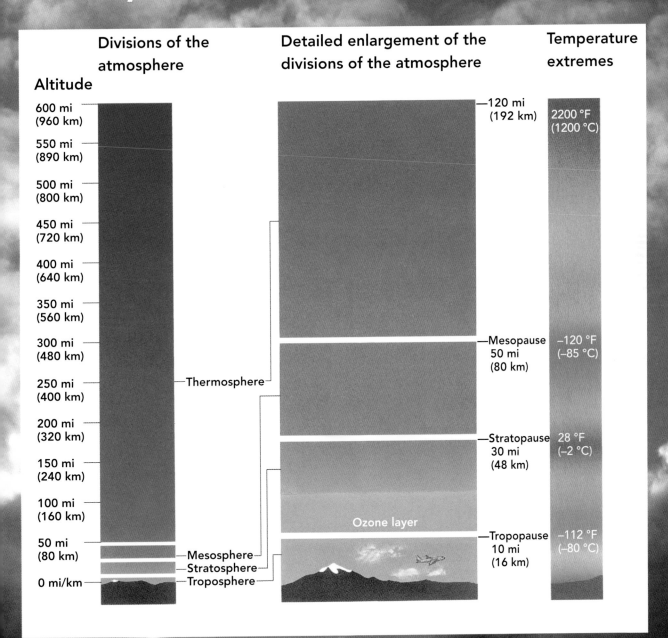

Divisions of the atmosphere

Detailed enlargement of the divisions of the atmosphere

Temperature extremes

Altitude

600 mi (960 km)	
550 mi (890 km)	
500 mi (800 km)	
450 mi (720 km)	
400 mi (640 km)	
350 mi (560 km)	
300 mi (480 km)	
250 mi (400 km)	
200 mi (320 km)	
150 mi (240 km)	
100 mi (160 km)	
50 mi (80 km)	
0 mi/km	

Thermosphere

Mesosphere
Stratosphere
Troposphere

120 mi (192 km)

Mesopause 50 mi (80 km)

Stratopause 30 mi (48 km)

Ozone layer

Tropopause 10 mi (16 km)

2200 °F (1200 °C)

−120 °F (−85 °C)

28 °F (−2 °C)

−112 °F (−80 °C)

What Is the Weather Like on Earth?

Earth has many types of weather. **Days** may be windy, rainy, snowy, cloudy, or sunny. Earth's weather takes place in the troposphere, the lowest layer of the **atmosphere**. That is because weather is caused by the movement of air, and almost all of Earth's air is found in the troposphere. Clouds form in the troposphere because nearly all the water moisture in the atmosphere is in this layer.

Heat from the sun is one reason air moves across Earth's surface. The sun warms some parts of Earth, such as regions around the **equator**, more than other parts, such as polar regions. The warm air rises and flows toward Earth's poles, carrying moisture with it.

As the air flows north or south, it cools, returns to the surface, and finally flows back to the equator. Earth's rotation on its **axis** also affects the weather. This spinning causes air to move.

Earth is not the only **planet** in the **solar system** with weather. But even the most violent storms on Earth's oceans and the coldest temperatures at the South Pole are mild compared with weather conditions on other planets.

Highlights

- The weather on Earth is much less extreme than the weather on other planets.
- Weather changes as air moves around Earth, carrying heat and moisture with it and creating winds.
- Warm air rises at the equator and flows toward the poles, where it cools and flows back to the equator.

Hurricane Katrina nears the Gulf Coast of the United States in 2005 in a natural-color photograph.

How Does Earth Move Around the Sun?

Earth *rotates* (spins) like a top on its **axis.** Earth takes 24 hours to spin completely around and return to the same position in relation to the sun. This time period for Earth's rotation is called a solar **day.** At the **equator,** Earth rotates at about 1,000 miles (1,600 kilometers) per hour. Earth's rotation speed slows the closer you go toward the poles. At the poles, the rotation speed is almost zero.

Like all the other **planets** in the **solar system,** Earth **orbits** the sun. Earth's orbit is **elliptical,** or oval-shaped. This orbit lies on an imaginary flat surface around the sun called the orbital plane. Earth's trip around the sun takes 365 days 6 hours 9 minutes and 9.54 seconds. This is Earth's **year.**

During a solar year, Earth travels about 584 million miles (940 million kilometers). Earth travels at about 66,700 miles (107,000 kilometers) per hour, or 18.5 miles (30 kilometers) per second, as it moves along its orbit.

Fun Fact

Because Earth takes about 365 ¼ days to travel once around the sun, every four years we have to add an extra day to the calendar—February 29. That is why we have "leap years."

The Orbit and Rotation of Earth

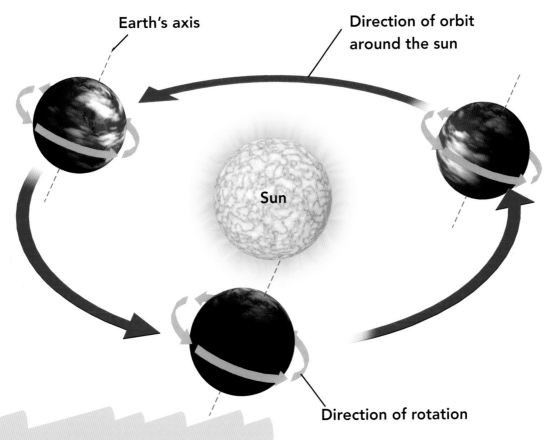

Earth's axis

Direction of orbit around the sun

Sun

Direction of rotation

Highlights

- Earth rotates on its axis at the same time that it orbits the sun.
- It takes 24 hours for Earth to spin once on its axis, the length of a solar day.
- It takes about 365 days for Earth to travel once around the sun, the length of Earth's year.
- Earth rotates most quickly at the equator and more slowly at the poles.

Why Does Earth Have Seasons and Climates?

Earth has seasons because it **orbits** the sun and has a tilted **axis**. As Earth travels in its orbit, one half of the **planet** is always tilted toward the sun. This part of Earth gets more sunlight. The sunlight also strikes the surface at a higher, more direct angle. Rising temperatures bring summer to the part tilted toward the sun. At the same time, the half of Earth tilting away from the sun gets less sunlight, and the sunlight strikes the surface at a low angle. This part of the planet has winter.

Earth's Climate

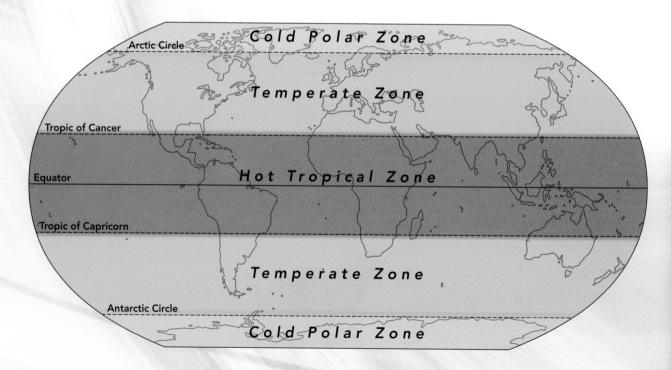

Earth's Seasons

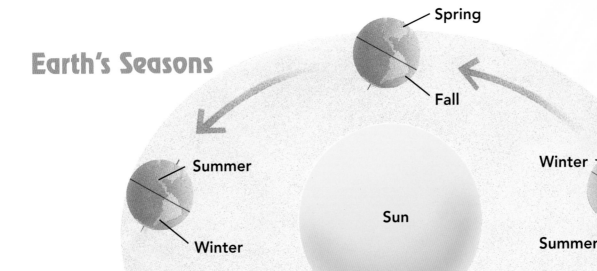

Spring

Fall

Summer

Winter

Sun

Winter

Summer

Fall

Spring

The seasons change as the amount of sunlight reaching various parts of Earth increases or decreases as Earth orbits the sun.

Earth's climate varies from place to place. Regions near the **equator** are always warm because they receive direct sunlight all year long. Areas around the poles are always cold because they get much less sunlight. The areas in-between have climates that are temperate—not too hot and not too cold.

Highlights

- Earth has a variety of climates because of the different amounts of sunlight that reach various parts of Earth.

- Areas around the equator are always warm because they receive direct sunlight all year long.

- Areas near the poles receive little sunlight and are always cold.

What Is Earth's Water Like?

Water is the most common substance on Earth's surface. It exists as a solid, a liquid, and a gas. Water fills Earth's oceans, rivers, and lakes. Water is in the ground and in the air we breathe.

Because Earth has mild temperatures, much of the **planet's** water is in liquid form. Liquid water covers about 71 percent of Earth's surface. Most of this water—about 97

In a natural-color photograph made by combining several images, Earth's water appears blue while the land is green and shades of brown.

Highlights

- Earth's water exists in three forms: solid, liquid, and gas.
- About 97 percent of Earth's water is salty ocean water.
- The rest of Earth's water is fresh water in streams, rivers, and lakes or is underground or frozen in icecaps at the poles.
- Water has chemical and physical properties not matched by any other substance.

percent—is salty ocean water. Only about 3 percent is fresh (unsalty) water. Most of Earth's fresh water lies under the surface as ground water or is frozen in icecaps around the poles.

Earth's water moves continuously from the oceans, to the **atmosphere,** to the land, and back to the oceans again.

This unending circulation of Earth's waters is called the water cycle.

Water consists of two **atoms** of **hydrogen** and one atom of oxygen. Water has chemical and physical properties not matched by any other substance. No other substance can do all the things water can do.

What Are Earth's Landforms?

Only about one-fourth of Earth's surface is land. Earth's landforms include mountains, valleys, and plains.

Mountains rise high above the surrounding land. Valleys are lowland areas between mountains or hills. Some valleys are narrow and deep, and others are shallower and several miles or kilometers wide. Plains are large areas that are generally flat. Plains that receive a lot of rain are often covered with forests. Grasses often grow on drier plains.

Scientists have used several spacecraft to map Earth's landforms in 3-D (three dimensions). These **probes** carry *radar* (an electronic instrument used to detect and locate objects) to collect information for a topographic map of Earth. Topographic maps are detailed maps that show the *elevation* (height above sea level) of land features as well as their position.

Highlights

- About one-fourth of Earth's surface is land.
- Earth has mountains, valleys, and plains.
- A number of spacecraft have used radar to map Earth in three dimensions, showing the heights of various landforms.

A 3-D map in false color, made by the space shuttle Endeavour

How Did Earth's Land Form?

Most scientists believe Earth began as a mass of rock. Over time, the interior of the **planet** melted because of pressure in the **core.** Certain chemical **elements** in the rock also gave off heat. Lighter rocks rose to Earth's surface and cooled, forming the earliest **crust.**

The mountains, valleys, and plains on Earth today formed over millions of years. Many were created because of the movements of the crust. The crust is not one unbroken rocky layer of "skin" covering the surface. Instead, it is made up of a number of separate sections called tectonic (*tehk TON ihk*) plates. These plates fit together like giant puzzle pieces.

The plates move about 4 inches (10 centimeters) a year—about as fast as human hair grows. The plates float on rock in Earth's **mantle.** This rock is so hot that it acts like a thick liquid.

Mountains and valleys often form at places where two tectonic plates meet. These plates can be pushing together, moving apart, or sliding past one another.

Highlights

- Many of Earth's features formed because of the movements of the planet's crust.
- Earth's crust is made up of a number of rocky pieces called tectonic plates.
- The plates move on top of a hot layer of Earth's mantle, shaping the landforms.

Mountains form where the edge of one plate plunges under the edge of another plate. Volcanoes and earthquakes are also common in these areas. In places where plates are moving away from one another, deep valleys may open up. Long chains of volcanoes can form where *molten* (melted) rock wells up between the separating plates.

At the San Andreas Fault in California (right), two tectonic plates are sliding past one another. A map (below) shows the location of Earth's main tectonic plates.

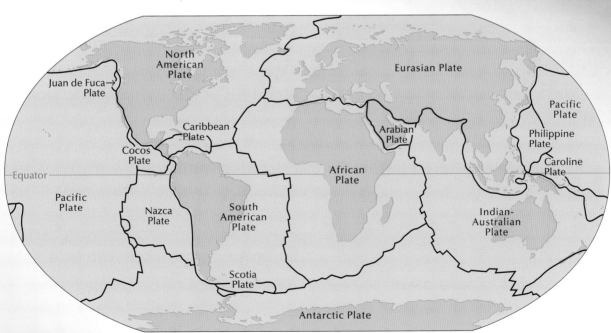

How Does Earth Support Life?

Earth is the only place in the **universe** that is known to support life. So far, scientists have not found living things on any other **planet**.

Earth **orbits** the sun in the habitable zone, also known as the "Goldilocks zone." Our planet's temperature is just right for life. It is neither too cold nor too hot for liquid water to exist on the surface. Liquid water is essential for life as we know it. All life on Earth needs liquid water to carry on life processes.

Earth's **atmosphere** contains gases that help make life possible. The atmosphere contains just the right amount of so-called green-house gases. These gases prevent

Highlights

- Earth's orbit around the sun puts it in the habitable zone, where the temperature is just right for liquid water to exist on the surface.
- The atmosphere helps to keep Earth warm enough for life.
- The atmosphere also contains the oxygen that animals breathe and the carbon dioxide plants need to make food.

heat from the sun that reaches Earth from escaping into space. As a result, Earth is warm enough for life. But Earth is not too hot for life to survive.

Earth's atmosphere also has the right mix of gases. It has oxygen, which animals must breathe, and carbon dioxide, which plants need to make food.

Some of the Varied Life Forms on Earth

Polar bear in the Canadian Arctic

Hawk with a captured catfish

A green turtle on a coral reef

Where Is Earth's Moon?

Besides the sun, the **moon** is the most visible and familiar object in Earth's sky. The moon is Earth's closest neighbor in the **solar system** by far. It is, on average, about 239,000 miles (385,000 kilometers) from Earth. The moon **orbits** Earth and travels along as Earth orbits the sun.

When viewed from Earth, the moon seems to "rise" in the east and "set" in the west. In fact, the moon orbits Earth in the opposite direction, from west to east. Earth also rotates on its **axis** from west to east. The moon only seems to move from east to west in the sky because Earth is rotating faster

Fun Fact

Besides the moon we all know about, Earth often also has several "temporary" moons—tiny objects that orbit Earth for a while and then fly off into space.

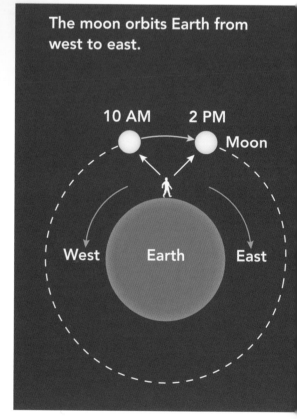

The moon orbits Earth from west to east.

10 AM   2 PM
                Moon

West   Earth   East

than the moon is orbiting Earth. You can see a similar effect on Earth when traveling along a highway in a car. Other cars may be traveling in the same direction—for example, going west. But if you are moving faster than the other cars, they will appear to be moving eastward, in the opposite direction.

Highlights

- The moon is Earth's closest neighbor in the solar system.
- The moon orbits Earth as Earth orbits the sun.
- The moon is about 239,000 miles (385,000 kilometers) from Earth.
- The moon appears to rise in the east and set in the west because Earth rotates from west to east.

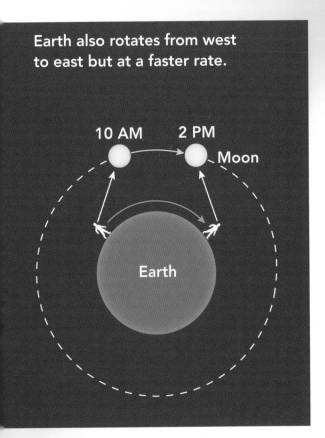

Earth also rotates from west to east but at a faster rate.

10 AM   2 PM
Moon

Earth

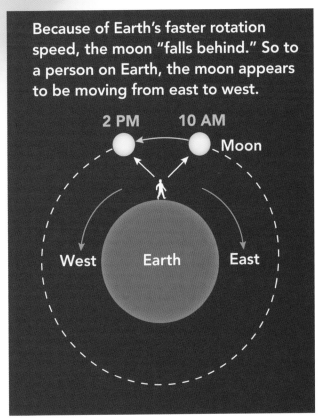

Because of Earth's faster rotation speed, the moon "falls behind." So to a person on Earth, the moon appears to be moving from east to west.

2 PM   10 AM
Moon

West   Earth   East

Earth and Earth's Moon 29

How Big Is the Moon?

The **moon** is much smaller than Earth. The **diameter** of the moon at its **equator** is about 2,159 miles (3,475 kilometers). This is only about one-fourth as great as Earth's diameter.

Because the moon is close to Earth, it seems to be about the same size as the sun. But the diameter of the sun is more than 400 times as great as the moon's diameter. The moon only appears to be about the same size as the sun because the sun is 400 times farther away from Earth.

Compared with the moons of most other **planets,** Earth's moon is fairly large. It is the fifth largest of all the moons in the solar system. The moons in the solar system that are larger than Earth's moon are Jupiter's satellites Ganymede—the largest moon in the solar system—Callisto, and Io, and Saturn's moon Titan.

Highlights

- The moon may look as though it is about the same size as the sun, but it is actually about 400 times smaller than the sun.
- The moon is larger than most of the known moons in the solar system.
- Jupiter's moon Ganymede is the largest known moon in the solar system.

The diameter of the moon
is only about one-fourth as
large as Earth's diameter.

What Does the Moon Look Like?

The **moon** shines with a silvery glow in the night sky. When seen by the unaided eye, the moon looks like a smooth globe with dark and light patches of gray on its surface.

When viewed with strong binoculars or a small telescope, the moon's **craters** and other surface features are easy to see. Features that appear as light patches of gray are actually rough, cratered highlands called **terrae** *(TEHR ee)*. The dark patches of gray are rocky lowlands called **maria** *(MAHR ee uh)*. The maria are covered with **basalt**—a hard volcanic rock. Volcanoes on the moon erupted billions of years ago. The lava they produced cooled and became solid, forming smooth rock. Maria look like dark bodies of water. In fact, the word *maria* is Latin for *seas*.

Highlights

- The moon's surface features are visible with a telescope or strong binoculars.
- Terrae, which appear light gray, are rough, cratered highlands.
- Maria, which appear dark gray, are rocky lowlands.
- The maria are covered with a rock called basalt, which formed when lava flowed from volcanoes on the moon and then hardened.

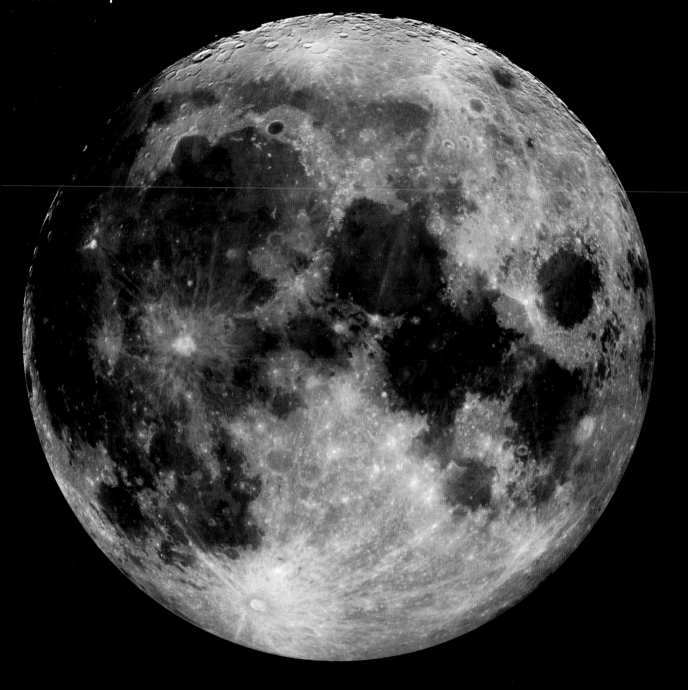

The moon in a
false-color photo

What Is the Moon Made Of?

The **moon's** surface is covered with a type of dark grayish soil called **regolith** *(REHG uh lihth)*. Regolith consists of dust-like bits of rock. Tiny **meteorites** smashing into the moon over billions of years formed the regolith.

There are two main types of moon rocks. **Basalt** is the hardened lava found in the **maria.** Breccia *(BREHCH ee uh or BREHSH ee uh)* is a type of scattered, crushed rock that is found mainly in the **terrae.**

Like Earth, the moon has three layers—**crust, mantle,** and **core.** The moon's strong outer crust is about 37 miles (60 kilometers) thick on the near side (the side that faces Earth) and about 50 miles (80 kilometers) thick on the far side (the side turned away from Earth). Scientists do not know much about the moon's interior. But they believe its **mantle** is rich in iron and magnesium. The **core,** which is made mostly of iron and nickel, is probably about 500 miles (800 kilometers) in **diameter.**

Highlights

- The moon has a strong outer crust, a mantle made of iron and magnesium, and a core made mostly of iron and nickel.
- The moon's soil, called regolith, is dark gray and made of dust-like bits of rock.
- The two main types of moon rock are basalt and breccia.

Inside the Moon

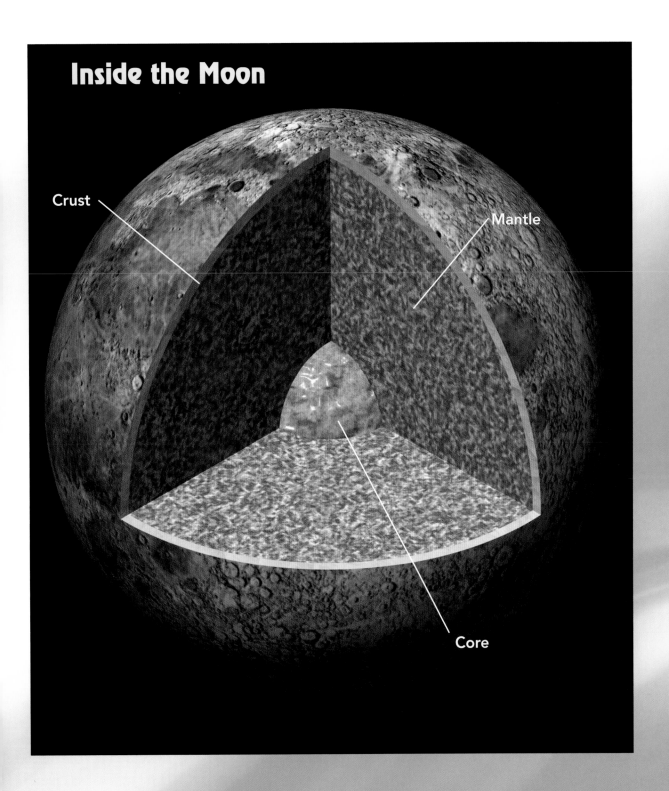

Crust

Mantle

Core

What Is the Surface of the Moon Like?

Probably the most familiar and spectacular of the **moon's** surface features are its millions of **craters.** Scientists estimate that hundreds of thousands of craters are more than one-half mile (0.7 kilometer) wide. The craters were formed as **meteoroids, asteroids, comets,** and other space objects collided with the moon's surface over billions of years.

Craters exist in many shapes and sizes. Younger craters are surrounded by matter that fans out from the center in a pattern that resembles rays of sunlight. These rays consist of **matter** that flew up when the crater was formed. Older craters have rounded edges that were worn down, scientists think,

Highlights

- The moon is covered with millions of craters.
- The craters formed when such space objects as meteoroids, asteroids, and comets struck the moon's surface.
- The moon also has winding channels called rilles that were formed by lava flows millions of years ago.

by the constant flow of energy and particles from the sun. Large craters sometimes have mountains in the center. These mountains are made of moon material that bounced upward after an impact.

The moon's surface also has valleys and winding channels called **rilles** (*rihlz*). Scientists suspect that running lava formed the rilles long ago.

Craters on the moon's surface in a black-and-white photo

A rock brought back from the moon by astronauts

How Does the Moon Compare with Earth?

You probably could not think of two objects in space that look much more different than Earth and its **moon.** Earth is a lush, warm, watery **planet** filled with life. Earth is also surrounded by a thick **atmosphere.** The moon is a lifeless desert with extremely hot or cold temperatures. Because the moon has no atmosphere, the sky always looks black.

The moon is much smaller than Earth, with a **diameter** only about one-fourth as large. The moon is also much less dense than Earth. The moon's **mass** (amount of **matter**) is only about 1/80 of Earth's mass. As a result, the pull of **gravity** on the moon's surface is six times weaker than the pull of gravity on Earth's surface. That means that someone who weighs 100 pounds (45 kilograms) on Earth would weigh only 17 pounds on the moon, the equivalent of 7.5 kilograms on Earth.

Highlights

- Earth is a planet with many features that support life, including water, an atmosphere, and moderate temperatures.
- Earth's moon has no atmosphere and its temperatures are extreme.
- Earth is much larger than its moon.

How Do They Compare?

	Earth	Moon
Size in diameter (at equator)	7,926 miles (12,756 kilometers)	2,159 miles (3,475 kilometers)
Average distance from sun (for the moon, average distance from Earth)	About 93 million miles (150 million kilometers)	About 239,000 miles (385,000 kilometers)
Length of year (in Earth days)	365.256 days	27.3 days
Length of day (in Earth time)	24 hours	29.5 Earth days
What an object would weigh ...	If it weighed 100 pounds (45 kilograms) on Earth ...	... it would weigh about 17 pounds (the equivalent of 7.5 kilograms) on the moon.
Number of moons	1	0
Rings	No	No
Atmosphere	Nitrogen, oxygen, argon	None

How Does the Moon Move Around Earth?

The **moon** travels around Earth at about 2,300 miles (3,700 kilometers) per hour. It takes 27.3 **days** to complete one **orbit** around Earth. The orbit of the moon, like Earth's orbit, is **elliptical,** or oval-shaped. Together, Earth and the moon orbit the sun. At the same time, both *rotate* (spin) on their **axis**. The moon rotates so slowly that it takes 29.5 Earth days to spin once on its axis.

Until space **probes** traveled to the moon, people had seen only one side of the moon, the so-called near side. The other side of the moon—called the far side—is always turned away from Earth. At one time in the distant past, all sides of the moon could be seen from Earth. That changed because one half of the moon weighs slightly more than the other half. Over time, the force of Earth's **gravity** slowed the moon's rotation, and the heavier side—which we know as the near side—became "locked" in place.

Highlights

- One day on the moon lasts about as long as one of the moon's years.
- The time it takes the moon to rotate once on its axis is about the same as the time it takes the moon to complete one orbit around Earth.
- Only one side of the moon, called the near side, faces Earth.

Fun Fact

The coldest spot in the solar system that scientists have measured so far is on the moon—NASA's LRO probe found temperatures of –400 °F (–240 °C) at the south pole in 2009.

A photo of the far side of the moon taken by the Japanese space probe SELENE (also called Kaguya) just before it was deliberately crashed into the moon's surface in June 2009

Why Does the Moon Appear to Change Shape?

You have probably noticed that the **moon** looks a little bit different every night. One night, it is completely dark and cannot be seen at all. A few nights later, it reappears as a thin sliver, shaped like a backward C. As the **days** pass, more and more of the moon becomes visible. Finally, after about two weeks, the moon appears full—a bright, round ball in the sky.

These different appearances are called **phases** of the moon. The moon's phases occur because of the moon's **orbit** around Earth and the orbit of the moon and Earth around the sun. When the moon is between Earth and the sun, it cannot be seen from Earth. At this time, the sun is not lighting the part of the moon facing Earth. This phase is called a new moon. When Earth is between the moon and the sun, one whole side of the moon is visible. This is called a full moon.

As the moon changes from a new moon to a full moon, it is said to be waxing. As the moon changes from full to new, it is waning. When the moon looks nearly full, it is a gibbous (GIHB uhs) moon. A moon shaped like a C or a backward C is a crescent moon.

Phases of the Moon

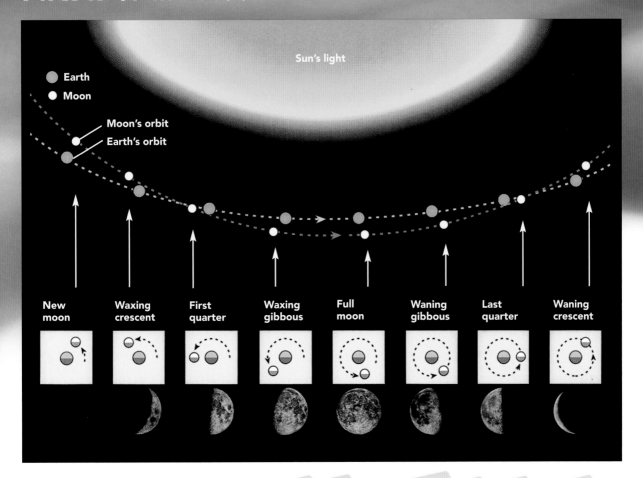

Sun's light

Earth
Moon
Moon's orbit
Earth's orbit

| New moon | Waxing crescent | First quarter | Waxing gibbous | Full moon | Waning gibbous | Last quarter | Waning crescent |

Highlights

- Changes in the way we see the moon in the night sky are called phases.
- The moon goes through phases because the position of the moon changes as it orbits Earth and as the moon and Earth orbit the sun.
- When the moon seems to be getting smaller, it is said to be waning. When it seems to be getting larger, it is said to be waxing.

How Does the Moon Make the Sun Disappear?

About twice a year, somewhere on Earth, people are treated to the sight of the **moon** blocking the light from the sun. This special event is called a solar **eclipse.** In a total solar eclipse, the sun disappears completely. Only a glowing halo of light shines around the moon to show where the sun is.

A solar eclipse occurs only during a new moon, when the moon is directly between Earth and the sun. When this happens, the moon—for a short time—blocks the light from the sun. The full shadow of the moon falls on Earth.

Total eclipses are visible only in the path of totality—that is, the area where the moon's full shadow falls on Earth. Because of the size of the moon and its distance from Earth, the path of totality is never wider than about 170 miles (274 kilometers). People who are outside but near the path of totality might see a partial solar eclipse. That means the moon does not completely cover the disk of the sun. People even farther from the path of totality will not see any sign of an eclipse at all.

Highlights

- The time when the moon blocks the sun is called a solar eclipse.
- A solar eclipse occurs when the sun, moon, and Earth all line up in a straight line.
- It is dangerous to look directly at the sun, even during a total eclipse.

Fun Fact

The moon is moving very slowly away from Earth because of forces created by the gravitational interaction between these two bodies in space. The moon is moving into a higher orbit at a rate of 1.6 inches (3.8 centimeters) per year.

A solar eclipse in Istanbul, Turkey

A Solar Eclipse

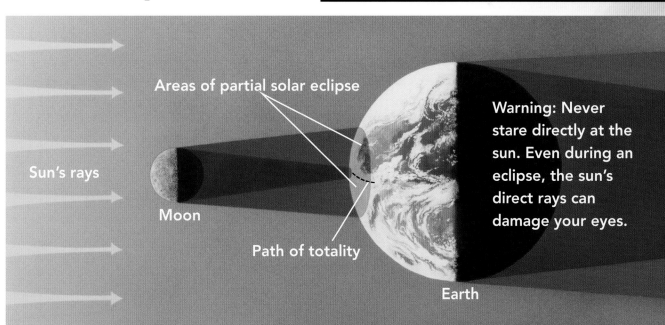

Sun's rays

Areas of partial solar eclipse

Moon

Path of totality

Earth

Warning: Never stare directly at the sun. Even during an eclipse, the sun's direct rays can damage your eyes.

How Does the Moon Affect Earth's Oceans?

If you have ever spent time at the seashore, you have probably noticed that the water level rises and falls throughout the **day.** This motion of the water is called the tides. Forces created by the gravitational attraction between Earth and the **moon** are largely responsible for the tides. The sun's **gravity** plays a much smaller role in determining the height of tides.

Gravity is the force of attraction between objects. This force is greater when the objects are closer together. The forces that create Earth's tides are strongest in the area directly below the moon and in the area directly opposite this location on the other side of Earth. In these areas, water in the oceans bulges out as high tides. High tide occurs in an area twice each day. As Earth rotates, the location of high tides changes.

The water in the oceans is at its lowest on the sides of Earth that are at right angles to the moon. These two areas are between the areas of high tides. On these two sides of Earth, there is low tide.

Highlights

- Water levels rise and fall along the ocean shore because of tides. Tides cause these changes primarily because of the force of gravity between the moon and Earth.
- The side of Earth that faces the moon and the opposite side of Earth experience high tides.
- The sides of Earth that are at right angles to the moon experience low tides.

Boats rest on the bottom of a harbor in the Bay of Fundy in Nova Scotia, Canada, during low tide.

As the ocean tide comes in, the water level begins to rise.

At high tide, there is enough water in the harbor for the boats to put out to sea.

How Old Is the Moon?

Scientists have concluded that the **moon** formed about 4.53 billion years ago, shortly after the formation of Earth and other **planets** in the **solar system.** Scientists calculated the moon's age by analyzing chemical **elements** in rocks and soil brought from the moon to Earth by United States astronauts and **probes** from the former Soviet Union.

Scientists also found that the chemical elements in the moon rocks were similar to those in Earth rocks. This indicated that the moon and Earth formed from the same material. How did this happen? Many scientists believe that the moon was formed after a huge object— about the size of the planet Mars—smashed into Earth.

After the impact, a gaseous cloud of rock flew off our **planet's** surface and began **orbiting** Earth. Over time, the cloud cooled into a ring of small, solid bodies. Eventually these bodies came together, forming the moon. As the small bodies collided and stuck together, they released a huge amount of heat. The new moon was probably covered by an ocean of melted rock.

Highlights

- Most scientists believe the moon was formed about 4.5 billion years ago.
- After studying Earth and moon rocks, scientists theorized that the moon formed after a collision between Earth and a large space object.
- The collision caused a cloud of material to fly from Earth's surface into space. There, the material cooled and hardened into the shape of the moon today.

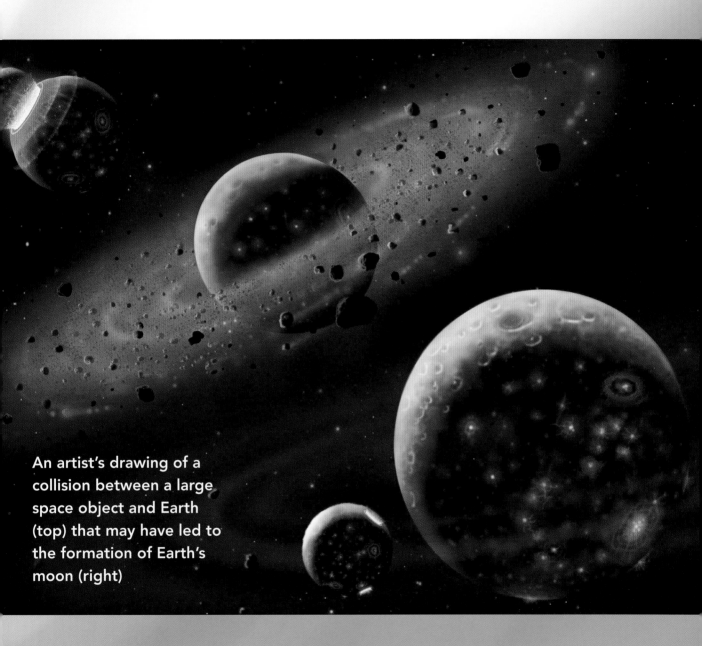

An artist's drawing of a collision between a large space object and Earth (top) that may have led to the formation of Earth's moon (right)

What Were the First Space Probes to Explore the Moon?

Highlights

- The first spacecraft to reach the moon was the Soviet Union's Luna 1, in January 1959.
- The first U.S. probe to visit the moon was Pioneer 4, in March 1959.
- The Soviet Union's Luna 3 took the first photograph of the far side of the moon.

The first space **probe** sent to the **moon** was launched by the Soviet Union, a large and powerful country that existed from 1922 to 1991. The probe, called Luna 1, passed near the moon in January 1959. The first U.S. lunar probe was Pioneer 4, sent in March 1959. In September 1959, the Soviet Union's Luna 2 became the first probe to crash into the moon's surface. In October 1959, Luna 3 photographed the far side of the moon—the side that faces away from Earth. It was the first time people saw what that side of the moon looked like.

In the mid-1960's, a number of U.S. and Soviet probes **orbited** and also made successful landings on the moon. These probes sent back pictures of the moon's surface and returned samples of the moon's soil. Many of these probes provided valuable information that allowed astronauts from the United States to land on the moon six times from 1969 to 1972.

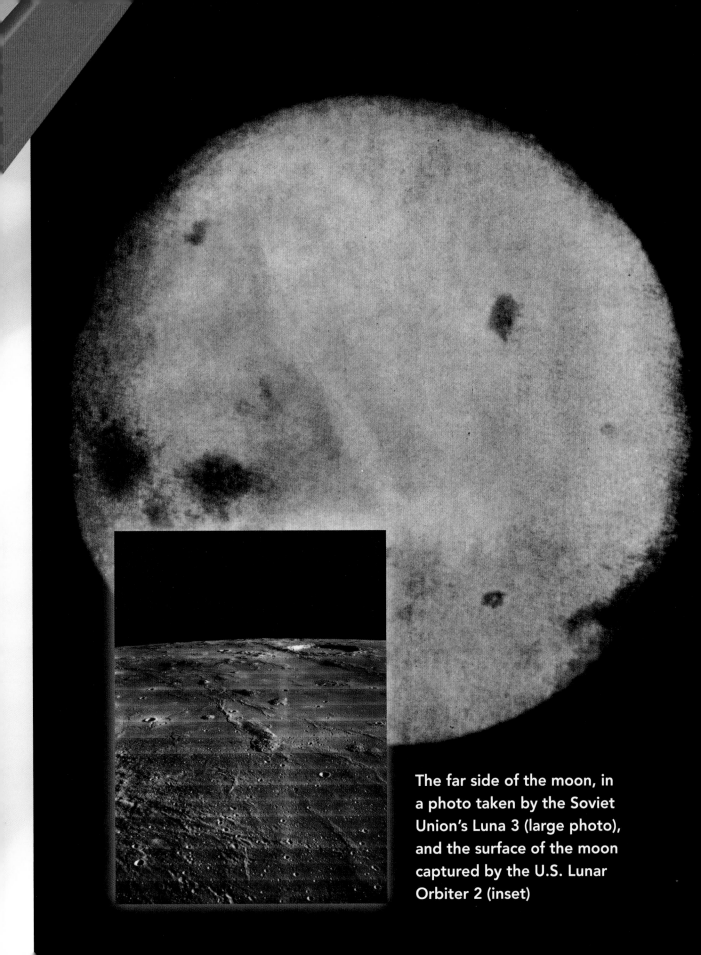

The far side of the moon, in a photo taken by the Soviet Union's Luna 3 (large photo), and the surface of the moon captured by the U.S. Lunar Orbiter 2 (inset)

When Did People Travel to the Moon?

In 1961, U.S. President John F. Kennedy set a goal to send astronauts to the **moon** before the end of the 1960's. Engineers with the National Aeronautics and Space Administration (NASA) began working on the project, which was called Apollo. They designed a spacecraft that would carry the astronauts to the moon and land on its surface.

In December 1968, astronauts from the Apollo 8 mission became the first to **orbit** the moon. The Apollo 11 mission successfully landed astronauts on the moon. On July 20, 1969, astronauts Neil A. Armstrong and Buzz Aldrin stepped out of the lunar module (landing craft) and onto the moon's surface. Armstrong was the first to set foot on the moon. His first words as he stepped onto the surface were, "That's one small step for a man, one giant leap for mankind." Five more Apollo missions landed astronauts on the moon after Apollo 11.

Highlights

- U.S. President John F. Kennedy set the goal to send astronauts to the moon.
- In December 1968, astronauts aboard Apollo 8 became the first to orbit the moon.
- Two astronauts with the Apollo 11 mission, Neil A. Armstrong and Buzz Aldrin, became the first to walk on the moon in 1969.

Buzz Aldrin walks on the moon (above). The lunar module (landing craft) is in the background on the right, and a United States flag stands at the center. A rocket launched Apollo 11 into space (right).

Will People Return to the Moon?

From the last **moon** landing in 1972 to the early 2000's, NASA and other space agencies concentrated on sending **probes** to other **planets** and on building space stations. In 2004, U.S. President George W. Bush called for American astronauts to return to the moon by 2020. President Bush considered a moon mission to be the first step in helping astronauts prepare for an even bigger mission—landing on Mars.

In some ways, the moon seems similar to Mars—dry, cold, and covered with dust. Scientists thought that if people could learn to live on the moon, they could more easily live on and explore Mars. To meet that goal, NASA launched the Lunar Reconnaissance Orbiter (LRO) in June 2009. The LRO **orbited** the moon, creating three-dimensional maps of its surface.

In 2010, however, President Barack Obama pointed NASA in a different direction. He urged

Fun Fact

What did Neil Armstrong *really* say when he stepped onto the moon? He said, "That's one small step for a man, one giant leap for mankind." But the "a" was lost in transmission, so for many years, people argued about what he actually said.

Highlights

- People have not landed on the moon since 1972.
- Beginning in 2004, NASA prepared to return to the moon. But in 2010, the agency's plans changed to developing technology for other types of missions.
- Many nations are still interested in learning about the moon, and one day, people may return there.

scientists to develop technologies that could be applied to a variety of future missions, not just living on the moon. Many other nations also continue to study the moon, and someday, people may once again walk or ride across its dusty landscape.

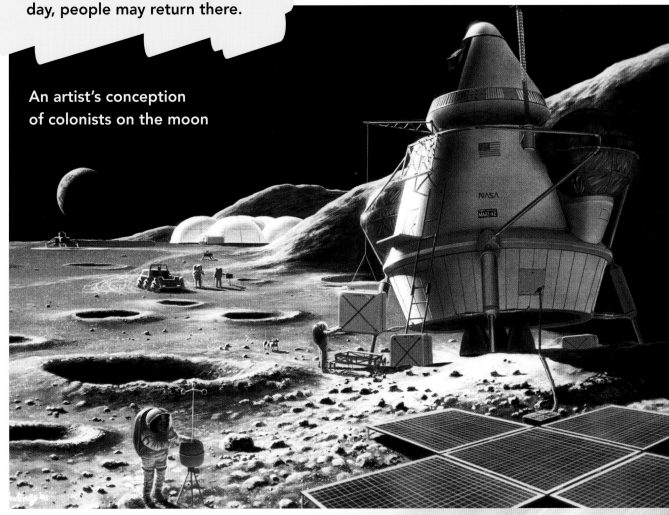

An artist's conception of colonists on the moon

What Have Probes Discovered About the Moon?

Space **probes** from several nations have flown to or past the **moon** since the last lunar landing in 1972. The European Space Agency's SMART-1 spacecraft **orbited** the moon from 2004 to 2006. It studied the moon's chemical composition.

Japan's SELENE spacecraft (nicknamed Kaguya) and China's first moon probe, Chang'e 1, both orbited the moon from 2007 to 2009, before crashing into the moon, as planned. These probes also studied chemical **elements** in the moon, and SELENE took the first high-definition television views of the moon.

A number of space probes have contributed to research about one of the most important findings about the moon—the presence of

A plume of debris (circled in red) rises from the moon as NASA's LCROSS probe intentionally crashes into a heavily shadowed crater in 2009. Scientists estimated that the plume contained about 25 gallons (95 liters) of water.

water and ice. The U.S. probe Lunar Prospector found strong evidence for ice at both of the moon's poles in 1999.

In 2009, NASA crashed the LCROSS probe into a **crater** near the south pole to look for water. Scientists reported that the cloud of dust kicked up on impact confirmed that the moon has a significant amount of frozen water. In March 2010, scientists reported that radar aboard Chandrayaan-1, India's first lunar spacecraft, had detected deposits of ice in more than 40 small craters near the north pole.

Most of the water on the moon (indicated in blue) is concentrated near the poles, as shown in a false-color image made by combining several photographs taken by India's Chandrayaan-1 spacecraft.

Could There Be Life on the Moon?

Scientists and astronauts have never detected any form of life on the **moon.** The moon lacks most of the conditions needed by living things, including liquid water and comfortable temperatures.

However, we know that the moon has at least some water and ice. The U.S. space **probes** Clementine in 1994 and Lunar Prospector in 1998 found strong evidence of water ice on the moon. The ice was found in **craters** at the moon's north and south poles, where the least amount of sunlight falls. Scientists believe that the ice was brought to the moon when **comets** crashed into it 2 billion to 3 billion years ago. NASA's LCROSS probe found water in the top layer of lunar soil in 2009. Could this mean that some form of life might be possible on the moon after all? Right now, scientists do not know for sure.

Highlights

- So far, scientists have not found evidence of life on the moon.
- However, U.S. space probes found some ice at the moon's poles and water in the moon's top layer of soil.
- The ice may have been brought to the lunar surface when a comet crashed into the moon 2 billion to 3 billion years ago.

The south polar region of
the moon in a black-and-white
photo taken by the
Clementine probe

Glossary

asteroid A small body made of rock, carbon, or metal that orbits the sun. Most asteroids are between the orbits of Mars and Jupiter.

astronomer A scientist who studies stars, planets, and other objects and forces in space.

atmosphere The mass of gases that surrounds a planet.

atom One of the basic units of matter.

axis In planets, the imaginary line about which the planet seems to turn, or rotate. (The axis of Earth is an imaginary line running between the North and South poles.)

basalt A hard, dark volcanic rock.

comet A small body made of dirt and ice that orbits the sun.

core The center part of the inside of a planet or moon.

crater A bowl-shaped depression on the surface of a moon or planet.

crust The solid, outer layer of a planet or moon.

day The time it takes a planet to rotate (spin) once around its axis and come back to the same position in relation to the sun.

diameter The length of a straight line through the middle of a circle or anything shaped like a ball.

eclipse An event that happens when the shadow of one object in space falls on another object, or when one object moves in front of another and blocks its light.

element A basic unit of matter that contains only one kind of atom.

elliptical Having the shape of an ellipse, which is like an oval or flattened circle.

equator An imaginary circle around the middle of a planet.

granite A hard, coarse-grained rock.

gravity The effect of a force of attraction that acts between all objects because of their mass.

hydrogen The most abundant chemical element in the universe.

mantle The area of a planet or moon between the crust and the core.

maria Broad, flat, dark areas on the moon.

mass The amount of matter a thing contains.

matter The substance, or material, of which all objects are made.

meteorite A mass of stone or metal from outer space that has reached the surface of a planet or moon without burning up in that body's atmosphere.

meteoroid A small object, believed to be the remains of a disintegrated comet, which travels through space.

moon A smaller body that orbits a planet.

orbit The path that a smaller body takes around a larger body, for instance, the path that a planet takes around the sun. Also, to travel in an orbit.

phase The shape of the moon or of a planet as it is seen at a particular time.

planet A large, round body in space that orbits a star. A planet must have sufficient gravitational pull to clear other objects from the area of its orbit.

probe An unpiloted device sent to explore space. Most probes send data (information) from space.

radiation Energy given off in the form of waves or small particles of matter.

regolith The layer of soil and loose rock fragments overlying solid rock.

rille A snake-like channel on the moon that may have been made by flowing lava. These channels wind across many areas of the moon's maria.

satellite An artificial satellite is an object built by people and launched into space, where it continuously orbits Earth or some other heavenly body.

silicate A group of minerals that contain silicon, oxygen, and one or more metallic elements. Silicates make up about 95 percent of Earth's crust.

solar system A group of bodies in space made up of a star and the planets and other objects orbiting around that star.

star A huge, shining ball in space that produces a tremendous amount of light and other forms of energy.

terra Part of the moon's surface that is not one of the maria. (The plural is terrae.)

universe Everything that exists anywhere in space and time.

year The time it takes a planet to complete one orbit around the sun.

For More Information

Books

Earth:

Earth by Elaine Landau (Children's Press, 2008)

Earth and the Universe by Ian Graham (Children's Press, 2009)

Earth's Journey Through Space by Trudy E. Bell
(Chelsea House, 2008)

What's So Special About Planet Earth? by Robert E. Wells
(Albert Whitman, 2009)

Moon:

The Moon by Elaine Landau (Children's Press, 2008)

Moon by Jacqueline Mitton (DK Publishing, 2009)

Web sites

Earth:

NASA'S Solar System Exploration: Earth
http://sse.jpl.nasa.gov/planets/profile.cfm?Object=Earth&Display=Kids

National Geographic's Science and Space: Earth
http://science.nationalgeographic.com/science/space/solar-system/earth.html

Moon:

NASA'S Solar System Exploration: Earth's Moon
http://sse.jpl.nasa.gov/planets/profile.cfm?Object=Moon&Display=Kids

NASA'S Lunar Science for Kids
http://lunarscience.arc.nasa.gov/kids/

Index

air. *See* atmosphere
Aldrin, Buzz, 52, 53
Apollo missions, 52-53
Armstrong, Neil A., 52
astronauts, 50, 52-54
atmosphere, 8, 12-15, 38; life and, 26;
    water cycle and, 21
axis. *See* rotation

basalt, 10, 32, 34
breccia, 34
Bush, George W., 54

Chandrayaan-1 probe, 57
Chang'e 1 probe, 56
circumference, 6
Clementine probe, 58, 59
climate, 18-19
clouds, 8, 14
comets, 36, 58
core: of Earth, 10, 11, 24; of moon,
    34, 35
craters, 32, 36, 37, 57, 58
crust: of Earth, 8, 10, 11, 24; of moon,
    34, 35

day, 16
diameter: of Earth, 6-7; of moon,
    30-31, 38

Earth: appearance of, 8-9; life on, 5,
    26-27; materials in, 10-11; moon
    compared with, 38-39; moon
    formation from, 48-49; orbit of,
    4-5, 16-19, 26; seasons and climate
    of, 18-19; size of, 6-7; water on, 8,

20-21, 26; weather on, 14-15.
    See also atmosphere; land; moon
earthquakes, 25
eclipses, solar, 44-45
elliptical orbits, 4, 16, 40
Endeavour (space shuttle), 23
equator: of Earth, 6, 14, 16, 19; of
    moon, 30
European Space Agency, 56

Ganymede, 30
Goldilocks zone, 26
granite, 10
gravity, 38, 40, 46
greenhouse gases, 26

habitable zone, 26
Hurricane Katrina, 14
hydrogen, 21

ice, 57, 58
inner planets, 4-5
iron, 5, 10, 34, 35

Jupiter, 6, 7, 30

Kennedy, John F., 52

land, 8, 22-23; formation of, 24-25
LCROSS probe, 56, 57
life, 5, 26-27, 58
Luna probes, 50, 51
Lunar Orbiter 2 probe, 51
Lunar Prospector, 57, 58
Lunar Reconnaissance Orbiter (LRO),
    41, 54

Earth and Earth's Moon 63